PTSD

The Ageless Disorder

Scott Blake

chipmunkapublishing

the mental health publisher

All rights reserved, no part of this publication may be reproduced by any means, electronic, mechanical photocopying, documentary, film or in any other format without prior written permission of the publisher.

Published by

Chipmunkapublishing

PO Box 6872

Brentwood

Essex CM13 1ZT

United Kingdom

http://www.chipmunkapublishing.com

Copyright © Scott Blake 2010

Chipmunkapublishing gratefully acknowledge the support of Arts Council England.

PTSD

Author Biography

Now in his fifties a generation has passed since the traumatic events that ruined his life. Scott was a company director when he had his mental breakdown. Subsequent to that he had counselling by a Community Psychiatric Nurse and Scott's past was discussed in great depth. It transpired that the traumas Scott faced all those years ago, when serving in the armed forces, had a terrible effect on him, unknowingly. That awareness of events long forgotten caused his life to completely change. Eight years after having the events exposed, in counselling, Scott was diagnosed with Post Traumatic Stress Disorder, which relieved Scott from the madness his world had become, and highlighted his set of symptoms defining his PTSD.

Divorced from his first wife who could not deal with Scott's behaviour, Scott lived several years on his own, until meeting his, now, wife Sarah, who has been inspirational in not only dealing with Scott's behaviour but understanding PTSD.

Scott has four grown up children from his first marriage and has discussed his illness with all of them in turn. They have all been understanding about the disorder and gone on, independently, to try and find out more about the illness. It was a result of their difficulty in finding U.K. based information that led Scott to write this book.

Scott Blake

PTSD

"Only the dead have seen the end of the war"

Plato 5 B.C.

I would like to dedicate this book to my wife Sarah, who as a Carer and wife has helped, and encouraged me to go on and complete the book

Scott Blake

PTSD

Introduction

So much has been said about post traumatic stress disorder and how it can affect a person in so many different ways. As a person who suffers with PTSD. I felt that it should be documented by a person who has lived with the problems of PTSD for many years in fact, to date, 32 years.

My first traumatic experience was in 1978 when I was 20 years old. My second traumatic experience was in 1982. Both events were totally unrelated and were as a result of my service in the Armed Forces.

How I became traumatized is not of great significance, it is the outcome of the traumas that I wish to concentrate on with in this book.

The book will deal with the fall out due to the traumas that I suffered with and will cover a range of subjects that effect sufferers of PTSD. It will cover the major problems that sufferers have to deal with and highlight the difficulties that sufferers have to face, in order to try and lead a normal existence.

The subjects vary from being diagnosed with PTSD, to trying to understand how life goes on around you and not being included because of PTSD. I will cover a day in the life of a sufferer as seen through my eyes which will highlight not only the symptoms being experienced, but also show how difficult it is to function normally, when there are people all around, who do not understand what a sufferer is going through. These people can range from general nursing staff to doctors and psychiatrists. I was alarmed when having to deal with front line professional personnel (doctors, nurses and surgery practice managers) who did not have any experience of PTSD.

From having my mental breakdown to being diagnosed with PTSD took eight years. In all that time I thought that I was mad and was beyond help.

I have decided to split the book into three parts. One part is for ex service personnel, one part is for civilians and the third part concerns subjects that are as a result of PTSD and can be problematic to all sufferers. It should be recognized that the majority of ex service personnel do not regard themselves as civilians. As the book will show, it is a running battle for them to try and understand the civilian way of life

The brain is affected in the same way, whether the person is civilian or ex service. Research has shown this to be the case and I will deal with this subject later on in the book. It is my objective in writing this book that the readers will be able to refer to a certain chapter which may be applicable to them. It has not really been written to be read from front to back, but even so, if the reader does this, I hope it proves to be an interesting read.

During my research for this book I was dismayed by the lack of information in the U.K., yet there is an abundance of material in the American market.

It is my hope, as well , that carers of sufferers with PTSD, will be able to understand a little more and realize that they are far from being alone , in looking after a sufferer.

Some of the ways in which a sufferer develops PTSD are heartbreaking as they can involve sexual abuse in both adults and children. People with learning difficulties who are unable to communicate their emotions need protection as they are in the highest range of vulnerability and its is for that reason they should be closely observed to check for any unusual emotions or behaviour, that have not been present before.

PTSD

Throughout the book I have used statistics to get a clear view of the enormity of the disorder. One particular set of statistics aside used concerning the judiciary system, I found to be most surprising. One third of those in prison today are ex service personnel. I am not saying that PTSD sufferers do not abide by the law, as the vast majority do, I am just trying to indicate the seriousness of having PTSD and show the way in which sufferers will go to, in order to hide away from the horrific memories, voices and hallucinations that go to make up their lives.

There has to be a time soon when PTSD is taken as a major problem for ex service personnel when leaving war zones .There is little to be gained by interviewing the service personnel as part of their leaving the forces routine. If they are suffering with PTSD they will probably not want to appear to be seen as weak, or they may be in denial (see Glossary of terms) Similarly there must be greater awareness of the problem of PTSD in normal civilian life.

If you find yourself becoming distressed when reading through this book it maybe the start of a natural healing process. If your stress levels increase further, or you feel they are at an unacceptable level put the book down and try to do something very different to distract yourself.

If, when reading this book, you feel you would like to use it as a work book and write how things are with you in any particular chapter, then I have left a gap at the end of each chapter for you to do so.

Scott Blake

PTSD

Part One

A typical day in my life

There is of course no typical day in any PTSD sufferer's life as every day will bring on a different set of challenges from the previous days. The resolve to be able to deal with these pressures can also change from day to day

Coming from a military background my PTSD centres around action in the armed forces.

I have two incidents of PTSD separated through the year by five months but four years apart. Both incidents are totally different to each other.

The latest I get up is 2.00am, if I have a reasonable night. This means waking up at least twice with nightmares. They are not that severe that I want to get out of bed. I set my alarm for2:00 am to wake up without having my final nightmare around 3 am which would drive me from my bed and start the day feeling dreadful.

If it is a bad night I can wake up at 12:30 am with such bad nightmares that I have to get out of bed and stay awake, fearful of any more frightening nightmares. In these types of nightmares I usually end up being burned to death and I smell the smoke and my burning flesh, from the fire and feel the pain of the heat. This type of nightmare will last from about the beginning of October until February depending on what the weather is like. The colder the weather the stronger the trigger is for these nightmares.

Depending on what time of year it is this can be replaced by an active combat service nightmare. These nightmares usually start around April and last until June. I am affected during the day by flashbacks and the triggers can vary from nightmare to nightmare.

I have probably had two hours interrupted sleep which is fairly normal for me .If the average person in the street was asked about the last time they had a nightmare they would be hard pushed to remember. PTSD sufferers can have several every night.

When I get up II make sure I ground myself. This is a routine I have become used to doing. It is a coping strategy recommended by a consultant psychologist I saw for about a year and it involves pointing at objects within the room and saying what they are out loud. I make myself a cup of tea which again is a grounding technique, as I use the majority of my senses when doing so.It concentrates the mind away from the nightmares.

I am instantly fully awake once the nightmares drive me from my bed and completely on guard.

I keep myself busy by using the laptop until everyone is awake probably around 6.30am.

I then take a shower which removes my tiredness and helps towards starting my day relatively refreshed by PTSD sufferer standards.

Throughout the day I will have visits, which are hallucinations, involving the victims, who talk to me as well, many times a day. The voices I hear are always blaming me for their deaths, being very derogative about me. The hallucinations do not care where or when they confront me, before I had to give up my driving license the hallucinations would appear sitting next to me in my passenger seat. Obviously this was extremely dangerous and I gave up my driving license voluntarily before having an accident due to the distraction.

PTSD

Because I am constantly tired I nearly nod off during the day and it is in that phase that I start losing touch with reality and talk with or try to touch the victims. I have asked countless times if anyone can see or hear the victims and of course they cannot.

I tread very carefully throughout the day avoiding trigger points that will send me into flashbacks. A smoking chimney or hot dog and burger bar. Sometimes just seeing someone in a wheelchair can send my brain racing back to tortuous times gone by. When this happens it seems like time has stood still. My flashbacks kick in and I do not know for how long I am transfixed by them. Over the years I have had people come up to me and ask if I am all right, so it must be some time for other people to notice my state and feel they should come to me, to see if all is fine.

There are a lot of everyday activities I cannot do on my own such as opening letters, answering the phone, answering the door, going anywhere on my own and going into shops, are just some of the problems I face . I fear that the worst will happen to me if I try to do any of these on my own. I have had panic attacks when trying to do these. I need constant reassurance.

In trying to improve my quality of life I have started two PTSD mutual support self help groups for civilians and ex forces people. Another ex service personnel group started in February 2010.

Depending on what day of the week it is I could be seeing my Support Time and Recovery Worker. She will take me into town and under my own pace, and confidence at the time, allow me to experiment by being on my own in town for a few minutes, usually walking to a pre-arranged Café that I am confident of how to get to. I find this time, usually one hour in total , difficult but very rewarding. It is quite common for me to have hallucinations and very derogative voices when I am trying to walk to the prearranged cafe. It is extremely difficult for me to try and walk unattended as not only do I have the PTSD problems, but I also have memory problems and quite often I will forget where I am. I always carry my mobile with me and I know my support worker's number in case I forget where I am or the PTSD problems become too intense for me to deal with on my own. By calling my support worker help will soon arrive.

Again depending on what week it is I see my Community P*sychiatric N*urse. I usually see her once a fortnight depending on how bad I am feeling. It can be once a week if I am going through a difficult time. This session lasts for about one hour and is an opportunity for me to talk about how I am feeling and what problems I have had since the last appointment. I can be so drained after these sessions that I am unable to do the simplest of things like making a sandwich without having to concentrate very hard to stop myself shaking.

I see my psychiatrist usually once every two months, but in my bad times this is once a month. It is obvious from what I have described that I am very fortunate with my support and I don't really know how I would cope without it. My psychiatrist is understands my PTSD and ensures that I have plenty of time to talk about how I am and how I have been since the last time I saw her.

Around the house

I am unable to do any cooking as I am afraid of any hot surfaces which induce a flashback. When I first left home I bought a microwave, as during my time in hospital I was given a flat to use before I found accommodation in the big wide world. I was told how to use the microwave and I wrote down how to, as I have to avoid anything to do with flames, which induce thoughts of people being killed.

PTSD

Going into public places I always choose off-peak times. For example going to the local cinema I always go in the afternoon, during the week, when I know that at best there is only a handful of other people watching the movie. I never go alone.

If I go away on holiday there is no respite as the voices and hallucinations, as well as the nightmares, follow me. It may take them a day or two to catch up with me, but they always do in the end. The only place I found where my voices did not follow me was when I attended a hearing voices group, so I could be guaranteed one hour every two weeks without my voices driving me down.

It has taken a great many years for me to be able to go out in public with someone else and not have consistent panic attacks, but it is only through sheer perseverance that I have managed to get to this stage in my recovery. I fully understand those sufferers who believe they will never be able to get out of the house and do the things that normal people do, because I was like that as well. It was a very painful journey to get to where I am now, and even then, I have only just scratched the surface of where ordinary people, without PTSD, can go and do.

I always do relaxation exercises before attempting to go to sleep and wish for a long and peaceful sleep. Then the cycle starts over again as if nothing has happened to me before and I wait for that refreshing shower in the morning.

I have included the transition from forces to ex forces and the difficulties it can bring, in order to show that life really can be a great hardship for the PTSD sufferer and the family. The word denial is used as a description for the time when the traumatic event has passed and the sufferer displays openly the symptoms of PTSD and hopefully has been diagnosed as having PTSD. It is odd looking back on my own life and thinking about the time I was in denial from the beginning of

1978 until my mental breakdown in 1994 I cannot remember thinking about the incidents at all. There were a lot of men who knew me during this time who had no idea at all that I had been through such life threatening situations, purely because it never occurred to me to mention it. It was if a cloud had covered the times of trauma preventing me from remembering such events.

With my first traumatic event there was a lot of publicity involved and I was in the media both nationally and locally. I even had a two-page spread in the Force's own newspaper yet when I was amongst my fellow colleagues nothing was ever mentioned. Looking back people may have been waiting for me to break the news of my rescue attempts.. The second traumatic event was of such great significance that it involved hundreds of men, I am bewildered, even today, to think I never once looked back at what I had experienced. Once again on returning to my base I acted as though nothing had happened.

The only real significance in surviving both traumas was that I became a very heavy drinker to the point where I used to drink myself to sleep. Once again it never occurred to me to try and understand this massive change in my behaviour. When I became a civilian I decided to work many long hours in an attempt to keep myself from thinking about how my life had been. It took my having a stroke and subsequent mental breakdown, which led to counselling by my community psychiatric nurse, to open up my Pandora's box and my belief that I was mad. I was in the mental health system for eight years before being diagnosed with PTSD.

I write this book therefore in the hope that someone who is or who knows of someone who has been displaying the symptoms of PTSD and to help them seek correct medical help. There may not be any cure for this terrible disorder but therapy and the appropriate prescription medication can certainly make life bearable at times.

PTSD

In writing a typical day in the life of a PTSD sufferer I have tried to portray my own routine. I have spoken to a lot of other sufferers within PTSD groups I have started, only to find we are very similar.

It is unbelievable to think that the human body can go with such little sleep for such great lengths of time as well as endure the punishments that the brain puts it under.

When I first told people who had never heard of PTSD that I slept for an interrupted three hours each night every night they found it implausible. It was only later when in the acute psychiatric wards would the staff, after heavily sedating me with the psychiatrists' prescribed drugs, witness my behaviour they became alarmed about my general health as well. When I talked to them about it and explained it was normal for me they became concerned. If the average person in the street was put through the same regime of sleep deficiency it would not take long for them to have major problems.

Leaving the Armed Forces

This book concentrates only on those suffering with PTSD. Over 80% of personnel leave the armed forces without PTSD and go on to have a full and satisfying life.

When dealing with leaving the armed forces I have split the subject into three. Married men and single men, as well as the problems associated with both types of personnel. The problems of having PTSD are so much more immediate with a married man than the single person.

Whereas the married man has great responsibility for his family, a single man has to try and stay within the system. Staying on the radar for the single man is of vital importance, because once he drops out of the system, there is very little that can be done to bring him back from a life sleeping on the streets as an alcoholic, drug taker. It may seem that I am being rather extreme in my approach when dealing with ex forces personnel, yet all I am trying to show is what the difference having PTSD can have on whether one is married or living alone.

I am using the sufferer as a male in my explanations but it could quite easily be female in today's sexual equality.

Not all marriages breakdown due to one of the parents having PTSD and also not all civilians end up on the streets I am just trying to illustrate that these are the possibilities and maybe some would say the probabilities that can happen.

Not everyone leaves the Armed Forces suffering from PTSD there are a great many who go on to live a normal life if only to be sensitive about their background, for example their regiment.

PTSD

Some ex forces personnel did not have the luxury of deciding when they would leave the forces. They were service no longer required. For these unfortunates the majority have probably the first signs, not recognized, of PTSD.

In the words of the song" into violent times one shouldn't have to sell your soul" Shout by Tears for Fears.

There are so many areas to be responsible for and if they are not done by the individual, they will probably not get done, leading to an extremely poor quality of life.

Humility after humility

Throughout this time it is highly likely that the ex service person could have been suffering with Post Traumatic Stress Disorder and has been in denial believing that this cannot be happening to them. When this happens then the real trouble of life begins.

There are around 17 different symptoms that make PTSD and it is not necessary to have all of them but every sufferer will be able to tick some off. The next stage is the hardest. Admission of an illness and worse still a brain related illness, and then seek help, It would never have been so in the forces.It would have taken great courage and only be ridiculed by fellow comrades.

Part Two

Married man leaving the forces

Whilst serving in the forces as a married man, most problems that make up the running of the home, are looked after by the MOD. The houses are normally rented and as a result maintenance costs are low with the tenant being able to call upon maintenance staff to resolve the problems.

It is the norm for a service person to have a married quarter as this does not involve having to put down a deposit for a mortgage. Whilst the forces pay seems attractive when joining up it does not spread far when there is a wife and children to support.

The pressure to stay on in the forces until retirement age is pretty heavy but it's is only a limited minority who actually manage to do so.

If someone had joined the armed forces in 1980 then there is a distinct possibility that they would have seen service in the Falklands campaign, Kosovo and the first Gulf war with service in Northern Ireland a probability .There would have been plenty of opportunities to see the horrors of war.

Whilst it looks good on the medal count, they do not mean much when trying for a job in civvy street. It is once again the isms that affect the likelihood of getting a worthwhile job paying reasonable wages. Then there's the property ladder to consider. There has to be something to show for all those years in the forces and moving into a council house would not normally be even considered

Trying to access this usually means starting at the first time buyer position. Not much house for a lot of money with interest rates to try and navigate around.

Whilst in the service there is the drinking culture, which is not affordable in civilian life, and the luxury of having a neighbourhood full of people in a similar position who all support each other, when husbands are at sea or away on manoeuvres for months at a time. There is also the fact that the married couples are not living in each other's pockets all of the time and the reunions are like honeymoons with the major problems not being addressed, the heavy drinking, for example. It is celebrating the return home.

In civilian life all is changed as the fight to sustain the household becomes number one priority despite investing services pension on the deposit of the house and the pension itself helping towards the monthly running of the household.

This does not preclude the married man who has done the full term of service having PTSD.

The symptoms of PTSD with a married man are far more desperate, as there are relatives involved wife and children, for example.

Just like any single person all the problems of getting a job still exist and to some extent awareness by the fact that the salary for the job has more importance, as it needs to try and keep the family in the manner to which they were accustomed whilst in the forces.

In this day of social equality it is still a fact that men over 40 years of age find getting a job more difficult than a younger man. If, having done the full term in the services, leaving the force there could well be the problem of ageism. The longer service personnel serve in the forces, usually the more difficult they find adjusting to civilian life, Rejection from interviews still hurts a great deal, if not more, as it is an embarrassment and pain to be seen as a failure.

Drink deadens the pain which of course eats into the monthly budget. With drink and rejection the money supply becomes less and then there are the rows. Sometimes violence ensues and possibly the breakup of the marriage and all the pain that brings. Sometimes the marriage survives, but under great strain and the symptoms of PTSD reveal themselves even more.

The spouse and children do not understand what is going on and the sufferer probably understands less, as they are enveloped with the disorder. It is a frightening time for all. A visit to the doctor usually results in medication for depression, in the hope that this will do the trick. It might do if that was the only problem, but as mentioned earlier, there are around 17 different symptoms of PTSD and it takes more than one to bring PTSD to the fore.

As time goes by and the symptoms worsen, that is if the sufferer has not had a breakdown, then the family members witness strange behaviour which is not helping the family financially.

The head of the family not being able to go outside, let alone to an interview, if lucky enough to get one. Problems opening letters, answering the door, talking on the phone, being able to drive, hearing strange voices and calling out to them, all frighten the family who do not understand what is going on. If the family is still lucky to survive to that stage then there is the repossession of the house due to lack of repayments on the small, but never the less, significant mortgage. The bed and breakfast life follows waiting for a place on the Council housing list.

There have been occasions when the spouse has actually taken the bull by the horns and gone to see their GP and insisted that depression is not the only symptom of the illness and something must be done. Perhaps an appointment with a psychologist is made unfortunately it is quite common for there to be over a 12 months waiting list. An appointment with a psychiatrist is more difficult not with the appointment time, but with the PTSD sufferer who would be stigmatized by going to such people for help. So the problem is compounded and the family breaks down as the drinking of the sufferer grows into unacceptable unaffordable levels.

Depending on the sensitivity of the spouse that PTSD sufferer may hear terms such as pull yourself together, grow up, or, stop acting like a child, words and phrases that strike to the very heart of the person suffering.

So the family breaks down and is split up with the children going with the mother who for this example is the spouse of the sufferer. It is important to note that women can suffer with PTSD as well.

Personal life takes a poor third place, if that, in some it doesn't figure it at all. How can a relationship form with someone who has no prospects and even less of a life being in control.

Once on the slippery slope to alcoholism or drug addiction, it is only a small minority that are actually fortunate enough to make something of their lives.

PTSD

Single person leaving the Armed Forces

Whilst in the forces single service personnel have all the problems of looking after themselves the forces it is if one has been unceremoniously booted out the back door and forgotten about in an instant.

There is so much to know and do.

How to fill in an application form, or write up a CV, and how to say the right words at interviews.

It is not very much for a prospective employee to just write ex army, for example, as that does not tell the employer much at all. The job centres hold courses on how to fill in application forms and write up CVS. If leaving the armed forces with PTSD and feeling totally unable to work, it is a great hurt to the pride when forms have to be filled in asking for Disability Living Allowance and Incapacity Benefit. To the applicant it feels as though they are asking for charity because they cannot work.

It is through my contact with Combat Stress that I was informed about being applicable for a war pension. This was carried out very sensitively with a doctor who understood PTSD coming to my house and asking me questions about myself, which I could answer in my own time and give as little or as much information as I felt able to do so at the time. My area representative from Combat Stress filled in the forms with me and sent them off for me, assuring me that all would be fine. I received a reply weeks later telling me that because of my PTSD I was to be paid a pension. This helped me financially a great deal and I am eternally grateful for the work my representative did for me.

If at the time of leaving the armed forces you feel as though you could go to work, there are possibly hours of paperwork and interviews to attend.

The dreaded interview, after countless letters.

Possibly the first time ever not counting the Careers Office.

Personal questions about life in the forces, having to stoop down to a civilian who would not have made the grade in the forces. How can there be respect?

Coming to terms with rejection. Why didn't I get the job?

More application forms and letters of rejection.

In this world of isms there could well be one for ex forces.

Changes in Lifestyle

Council flat refurbishment and furnishing, will probably have to be done, not like the forces where it was all done for you.

Feeding yourself and paying the bills are complicated enough for most people but when suffering from an illness, like PTSD, things can go pear shaped pretty quickly.

Not the same amount of cash in pocket or savings accounts, now a very limited lifestyle.

Embarrassment of situation of living on own, probably this is the first time having to manage a tight budget.

Moving in different circles can lead into a drug culture. Addiction of drink and or drugs but not admitting to it. The violence starts when defending what one has become.

Too much regular violence and getting known to the police can lead to prison or Community service, which is the ultimate in humiliation and is degrading because of former Forces status.

More exposure to drugs and violence.

Criminal with prison record.

This leads to a downward spiral towards homelessness for the better opportunity of three square meals a day in an institution with rules and regulations attracts sufferers. Prison.

A statistic

There are about 8000 ex forces personnel in prison today. With a further 16,000 more in the Judiciary system. It doesn't have to be this way.

Eventually they do come to terms with life.

It is a fact that more combatants have killed themselves since the Falklands than those who died during the conflict.

For some the transition to civvy street is less dramatic, living with parents or loved ones can take the financial pressure away from them but the price they pay is living with civvies that cannot see you have returned from combat and are living through the torment.

Part Three

PTSD

Researching into PTSD I found there is very little documented records of a sufferer's life, so I did not know whether it was unusual for me or the same for fellow sufferers. I came across Combat Stress an organisation that supports ex service personnel.

Upon my first visit to Combat Stress in Surrey I become convinced that I was not alone with my sleeping patterns when at 2 am on my first morning I went into the lounge and found it full of fellow sufferers who didn't sleep either.

I realized from conversations with fellow sufferers that I was extremely lucky to have the level of support I was being given, not only in quantity but quality. There are a many PTSD sufferers who get very little, if any, support at all. One must always remember that sufferers of PTSD are quite often, but not always, unreliable when it comes to appointments. This is not because they do not want to go to the appointment it is because they simply cannot because of their condition. Once again I am very fortunate that my support worker and my CPN come to my house for the appointments. When I see my psychiatrist I always invite my CPN to the appointment so that she can listen to what my psychiatrist asks me as well as helping me remember how things had been since the last time I saw my psychiatrist. My memory is very unreliable.

It was during my summer months, which are my least troubled time, that I set up a PTSD self-help group ,with the aim of being able to listen to and share in each other's problems and progress .This has been found to be a very useful resource for the members so much so that I formed a second group ,further away from my local town. This has been met with a lot more regular attendance to the extent where I am deliberating whether to subdivide the group into male and female groups .I was approached by Combat Stress to participate in the setting up of a local ex service PTSD group and hopefully this will be happening very shortly. This has given me a sense of achievement but I have kept my feet on the ground and keep reminding myself that I must not overdo things as it would probably make me even more unwell.

I was once invited to attend an all ex service personnel PTSD group and was quite taken aback by the amount of anger and frustration that they all seemed to feel. I believe that if I'd been a non ex service personnel onlooker I would have been a focus for their anger. The atmosphere within the group was totally different to that found within my local PTSD groups, which are mainly made up of civilians. The ex-service personnel were quite puzzled when I told them I had civilians in my group, they could not believe that without being in the forces it was possible to have PTSD. It really surprised me that they did not regard themselves as civilians and that PTSD belonged, only, to those who had seen action in the forces.

PTSD

Perspective

For everyone who has depression there Is a different reason. Likewise for everyone who suffers with PTSD there is a different reason.

It is quite interesting to note that whilst discussing the Falklands campaign and the Iraq war two PTSD sufferers came together and acknowledged they were both in different wars. One was in the Royal Navy the other in the Army.

The ex-army guy relates to the time when during the Iraq war how he had to protect himself from possible incoming SCUD missiles and wished he was on board one of the Royal Navy ships for protection.

The ex-Royal Navy guy was telling his colleague that during the Falklands campaign he wished he was on land to protect himself against the incoming enemy fighters.

This goes to show that even though they thought the other place was safer they were both sitting targets in certain situations.

There is no one who is indestructible at all times. Everyone has their vulnerable times.

From an article on 28th January 2010 by the Mental Health Foundation.

In a new policy briefing the Mental Health Foundation today called for more to be done to look after ministry veterans. Although the MHF welcomes recent initiatives to expand their mental health policy available to veterans it believes that support still remains patchy and that several critical factors still need to be addressed. Younger veterans must be protected from suicide, the over representation of veterans in UK prisons properly investigated and the link between alcohol misuse and poor mental health must be prioritized says the mental health of veterans.

Younger veterans at risk

Resettlement packages for veterans returning to civilian life should be based on need not just length of service says the charity. Veterans under the age of 24 are two to three times the risk of suicide than civilians of the same age. Despite this, the forces resettlement package for former forces personnel is only available after six years of service. The mental health of veterans calls for the Ministry of Defence to consider how support for younger veterans could be enhanced, so that vulnerable young people leaving the forces are properly protected.

Veterans in prison

In the light of recent research which found that twice as many veterans are in prison than British troops are in Afghanistan, the mental health foundation says that more research into what prevents veterans from returning to civilian life successfully is needed. Given that around half of veterans in prison are suffering from PTSD or depression, it is clear that more needs to be done to help veterans stay well and out of trouble says the foundation.

Concern over alcohol misuse

The high prevalence of alcohol misuse among veterans and service personnel, thought to affect one in five, is a particular concern says the MHF. Alcohol misuse services are currently very stretched and do not always work effectively with mental health services. The mental health of veterans calls for commissioners and providers of services to provide appropriate treatments for a range of disorders among veterans, including alcohol misuse.

Simon Lawton Smith, head of policy for the foundation said

"Whilst most members of the forces rejoin civilian life successfully, a significant number will struggle. There have been recent initiatives to improve the help offered to these veterans, both of these are not widely available and we feel it is particularly urgent that the support, those with alcohol misuse problems and those with alcohol misuse problems and those that at risk of offending are improved.

"we cannot turn the armed forces personnel where young veterans are twice as likely to take their own life than their contemporaries and prisons are full of veterans suffering from depression and PTSD".

The briefing outlines the background to mental health problems, the level of mental health problems they experience and the challenges veterans it can face in civilian life and details the supposed country available.

The Government's recent new horizons mental health strategy makes a commitment to review the needs of serving personnel and veterans. Veterans' mental health is also a priority for the improving access to psychological services (IAPT) program. However many areas still lack appropriate accessible services for veterans.

Mental health problems most frequently cited by veterans are depression and anxiety as well as substance abuse problems and PTSD.

Research suggests that common mental health problems affect about one in four service personnel and veterans.

While most veterans do not develop mental health problems as a result of serving those that leave the forces with mental health problems, often do badly and many do not receive help.

Veterans have cited the lack of understanding of the forces background from civilian services as a key barrier to seeking and receiving support. The mental health of veterans say there is a strong case for veterans to be involved in the training of health professionals who come into regular contact with veterans.

While the mental health of serving personnel is provided by the defence medical service , veterans are not entitled to this support and receive treatment through the NHS.

More needs to be done to ensure that veterans themselves do not see mental health problems as a sign of weakness. Veterans who could be the target of local health promotion initiatives and the case is strong for veterans to be involved.

PTSD

Ever since there has been conflict there has been a mental health problem, which we know today as post traumatic stress disorder.

The problem was documented as early as the American Civil War from what was known as Soldiers Heart, or Da Costa's Syndrome.

The First World War brought to the attention Shell Shock which was not accepted by the medical professions. Sufferers being thought of as malingerers, there is evidence that sufferers deserted , whilst others failed to obey direct orders.

Recently as many as 300 soldiers were given a full and unconditional pardon after being shot for their actions due to Shell Shock during the First World War.

The Second World War brought to light Battle Fatigue, yet another description of a mental illness because of exposure to combat.

It was first described as Post Traumatic Stress Disorder during the Korean War and more intensely during the Vietnam War. It is estimated that 860,000 American soldiers suffered with varying levels of PTSD. In 2004 a survey was done on ex veterans and it was found that at least 30% of sufferers still claim benefits and between 60 to 80% have developed an alcohol problem.

The average length of time in denial of suffering with PTSD is 14 years with the symptoms being masked by an abuse of alcohol or drugs and having to steal to feed the addiction.

To some sufferers of PTSD it is like a badge of honour, whilst for the vast majority it is a badge of shame. I know that in my case it is a badge of shame despite all my efforts in setting up new PTSD self help groups, to help other sufferers.

Although I did not understand why at the time, I declined medals awarded to me as I did not want any reminding of what I had been through. This met with a lot of opposition, from senior officers and comrades, believing I was being disrespectful to those who had given up their lives.

I must admit that as a general feeling the Falklands Conflict left a very sour taste with a lot of service personnel, as they viewed it as Thatcher's war and not fighting for Queen and country. It was a conflict where neither side had declared war on each other and could have been avoided, hopefully, diplomatically.

PTSD

COMBAT STRESS in Leatherhead treats ex armed forces personnel with treatments for:

post traumatic stress disorder

clinical depression

anxiety states

adjustment disorders

obsessive compulsive disorders

bipolar

substance abuse dependency such as alcohol and drugs

psychotic conditions

anger problems

many personnel suffer with more than one condition this is known as co morbidity

all the above are complicated by relationship and home life difficulties

In the July 2009 edition of Defence Focus, Combat Stress was stated as caring for around 4000 veterans and last year received 1257 new referrals an increase of 8% on the previous year and an increase of 66% since 2005. 60% of all seeking help are suffering with post traumatic stress disorder.

HELP FOR HEROES spend every penny possible making grants that aim to provide practical direct support for our wounded. The current focus is for grants to create a series of regional recovery houses to be built across the UK and serve as the last stage of rehabilitation before serving personnel return to their unit or transits back into civilian life.

Survivor's Guilt

This is the guilt that comes from the belief that my actions or non actions during my traumatic events may have caused or could have prevented death and injury. Survivor Guilt occurs because I believe I should have experienced death or injury myself, but escaped my fate.

Since those times I have had nightmares about those that died and were very badly injured and have felt guilt and sought direct and indirect ways of ways to kill myself in order to take their place.

Trauma and emotional health

A person who has experienced complex PTSD tend to either be too dependent on others in an intimate relationship or so terrified by any Intimate connection that he or she flees from such a relationship to aloneness. However when alone the survivor often feels an unbearable sense of abandonment and again longs for connection . When a survivor tries to connect and again becomes terrified of rejection and abuse. Their relationships begin to take on a pattern of being too close and running away.

Exposure to complex PTSD can prevent attaching in a healthy way to others. It may cause an inability to control emotional arousal. In a matter of milliseconds the survivor may go from being okay to being in a rage. They may also find that they do not have enough trust in others or themselves to allow themselves a stable relationship. Instead they may become aggressive towards others either publicly or in a more subtle, passive form as well, and towards themselves when things don't go their way. A complex PTSD sufferer may lack a predictable sense of separateness from others, have a disturbed body image, or have poor impulse control and become suspicious and distrusting in social situations.

Foreshortened Future

If you have basic psychological needs for safety, trust, power, intimacy which cannot be met adequately by you the world or others, then finding the reason may be a difficult task. You may believe that you are destined to live a very short life and that you will never live long enough to find peace or joy. This is called belief in a foreshortened future and it is one of the benchmark symptoms of PTSD.

PTSD statistics

Combat related PTSD occurs in every war

A 2005 study of the Korean War by Australians showed over 30% still suffered with PTSD

Over half a million soldiers in Wold War II suffered Battle Fatigue an early description of PTSD

In a study in 2000 over 25,000 ex service personnel from World War II, still claimed disability pension.

Britain recently issued pardons for over 300 soldiers of World War I who suffered what is now known as PTSD

PTSD affects more people than those who have asthma or diabetes in the USA.

Between 60 to 80% of Vietnam veterans suffering PTSD also have an alcohol problem.

Over 8000 off British prisoners are ex service personnel with a further 16,000 in the judiciary system.

It is estimated that between 15 and 29 % of veterans of Iraq and Afghanistan will suffer from PTSD

There are more ex service personnel in the Judiciary system than are serving in Afghanistan.

PTSD

Facts about PTSD

Combat service personnel run the highest risk, but anyone involved in a traumatic event can suffer with PTSD.

Brave people do not have a magic wand to fend off PTSD

Without therapy and medication PTSD will not be kept to a manageable level

Therapy can make your life better but not perfect

Try not thinking about it !!!!

There is something called denial (see Glossary of terms)

In reality it is the minority that are violent

The symptoms can present anytime and many times during the day.

Night times are particularly difficult due to nightmares and loss of sleep

It is both biological and physiological.

The levels of the reactions to trauma

Normal stress reaction

The feelings experienced with normal stress reactions can be the same as those suffered with PTSD, anxiety, fear, terror, anger, shock, grief etc. These feelings can be very powerful but can last a few days, weeks or even months. The important point to note that is that they do not stay at the same intensity or become worse.

Acute stress disorder

Starts within four weeks of the trauma, lasts between two days and a month and is so severe it interferes with a person's ability to handle normal day to day activities. In reality it is difficult to diagnose, as Normal stress reaction or PTSD. This time period is significant as if it lasts longer than a month it might well be PTSD.

Dissociation

Feeling spaced out, the world seems unreal, time speeds up or slows down, like watching a movie rather than living a life, emotions turned off and there is amnesia about large parts of the trauma.

Severe anxiety

Strong desire to avoid people, places or things associated with trauma. Flashbacks.

Post traumatic stress disorder

A much more powerful response and does not go away. Diagnosed if lasting more than one month, it seriously **interferes** with life and lasts a long time. Two main types:

PTSD

Simple PTSD starts after a single event.

Complex PTSD occurs when experiencing repeated traumas. Childhood abuse and wartime traumas are some of the triggers.

Acute post traumatic stress disorder

When symptoms last less than three months.

Chronic post traumatic stress disorder

When duration of symptoms is greater than three months.

Delayed post traumatic stress disorder

When symptoms do not start until weeks or months after a trauma.

It is important to note that there is a **denial** period , usually, which masks the effects of PTSD. This can last for many years.

Dealing with your perpetrators

For example if one has been sexually abused.

Dealing with complex PTSD involves alterations in perceptions of the perpetrator. One major aspect of this condition is adopting distorted beliefs held by the perpetrator as your own. These beliefs are called introjects. Another aspect is idealisation of the perpetrator. Many victims continue to idolise the perpetrator because the message is instilled in them. If you realistically look at the percentages of responsibility for a trauma that you had, the tendency to idolise the perpetrator would be less.

Many trauma specialists have written about the trauma victim's need to forgive their abuser. Forgiveness supposedly is a way to release the rage and hate that you have towards your perpetrator as well as a way to release your desire for revenge. Many offenders do not deserve unconditional forgiveness. Many also will not even admit that they have done wrong and therefore they do not seek or want forgiveness as it is not necessary for something that was not bad.

Forgiveness can be seen as the wilful abandonment of resentment and the willingness to respond towards your perpetrator with compassion, generosity and moral love.

What does this mean? It does not mean that you condone or excuse what has been done to you and what has happened in your world. It does mean a change in your internal response.

Forgiveness is not about granting your perpetrator a pardon, leniency or mercy, it does not mean you excuse that trauma, forget the offence or abandon resentment.

Forgiving your perpetrators may allow you to let go of your anger and rage to some degree. However, it is more important that you forgive yourself for any perceived complicity in what happened. Letting go of anger through forgiveness can help you let go of it at least some of the power your offender has had on you. People involved in domestic abuse:

On average:

8 1% of victims are female with male perpetrators one in four women and one in six men are assaulted by (ex) partners

A woman has been assaulted 35 times before reporting it to the police

Two women a week are killed by (ex)-partners

In times of war the opposing forces are not to blame for their actions just as you are not to blame for yours. You are doing what you are trained to do. Those to blame are the politicians and chiefs of staff for making those decisions that took you to war in the first place. If anger is an emotion that cannot be rid of then aim that anger not at the common man but at those who took you to war in the first place.

Dealing with psychologists and psychiatrists can be seen as a great sign of weakness by ex have made the right move. The professionals are there to help and will do all they can to help the sufferer.

I have explained a little about what goes on inside the brain causing those with PTSD to act the way they do. By doing this I have hopefully shown that with the appropriate therapy and medication life at times can improve for the sufferer.

I am not a medical man by profession, but I can understand what has been described as happening in the brain of a PTSD sufferer and how we differ from the average person. There is hard medical proof that there are abnormalities that cannot be changed purely by wanting them to.

Trauma relating to being stalked

Imagine walking down the road one day and stopping to buy a newspaper, casually looking around and noticing a face from the past looking the way before you glance eye to eye.

A first reaction might be thank goodness for that I didn't fancy talking to him after what we have been through in the past.

Further on down the road you stop to buy some flowers and there he is again quickly looking away before your eyes meet. Coincidence?

Finally getting home you put the key in the lock, look around and see him again. Not much of a coincidence now.

Being tired after a stressful day you let it pass.

The next day a letter is slipped under your door and it is from your old flame who you think you might have seen the day before. How does he know this address? I have moved since we split up. We split up because he was trying to wrap you in cotton wool and exclude you from your friends. He wanted you all for himself, he was far more serious about the relationship than you ever were.

The note reads of an apology and asks for a date to show you he has changed and should both get together to sort out the old problems. A mobile phone number is left. What should you do?

Confront him?

Go to the police?

Dismiss it as an act of stupidity on his behalf?

PTSD

Agree to meet up with him to sort things out?

Change a walk to work route?

All the above have their own merits but when the emotion of fear is involved, remember how angry he got when you finished the relationship?

Keep your distance and do not give him any room for encouragement. Go to the police and tell them the history. There is a good website www.safehorizon.org . Stalkers feed off the slightest bit of attention so it is important to ensure that there is no indication of this at all. If matters are not nipped in the bud quickly, full-blown PTSD can develop as a stalker takes over your life.

Changing the route to work can also help, different time, different transport, or bus number etc. It is important to remember these people are ill themselves.

Witnessing a traumatic event

The victims of a traumatic event are not just those that were involved in it, but also the unfortunate people who saw the event themselves and did not receive any physical injuries. The emergency services are a prime example of this although not witnessing the event as it happened they have to deal with the immediate aftermath. The dead, dying and horrifically injured plus the chaos of the incident

Doing their job in the professional way they are trained to, it is only hours, days later when they have time to contemplate what went on. In some cases reports have to be written which, for the writer, can cause trauma in itself. Watching videos of the aftermath for training purposes only goes to re live the true horror of what they were involved in.

The emergency service personnel are not superheroes, they have feelings just like everyone else, they are bound to be affected in some way.

In some ways the emergency services are just like an extension to the armed forces in dealing with such horrors, as they are quite often overlooked by the general public when it comes to the unimaginable scenes they have to work through.

A well documented case is that of the biggest bombing in Northern Ireland. The Fire Service were shovelling up body parts that were the result of a devastating bomb blast. How can anyone be supposed to be unaffected by that?

As mentioned previously the Kings Cross rail disaster. 100 people were actually involved in the tragic event, but over 600 were believed to have been affected.

Having personally been a witness to and involved in traumatic events I know from experience that those memories have

PTSD

stayed with me for over 30 years .In some cases I still relive those moments as if it was the day they happened.

I smell the scene, the people present, alive and dead and hear what was going on as if I'm going through the horrific events today. Some psychiatrists have said the lucky ones died and that people like myself are the real victims, who relive the horrors every day and night.

An interesting point that has come out of witnessing a traumatic event, is that usually no two accounts are the same. They are all from a different angle and different set of emotions.

Symptoms of PTSD

Re living the trauma. Going over the trauma countless times, trying to change the outcome.

Flashbacks. Unexpected reliving of the trauma with smell, sight and sound.

Nightmares. Being at the trauma and waking up usually screaming and thrashing about when the episode becomes too much to deal with.

Avoidance. Trying to ensure that any trigger points for the trauma are avoided e.g. smoke

Difficult to relax (constantly on guard). Instantly awake and waiting for something associated with the trauma to occur.

Easily startled. Heightened state of readiness for something bad to happen, in a different world where only the trauma exists, when touched or shouted at brought back into the real world.

Trying not to feel anything. In readiness to defend against trauma.

Feel detached or isolated from others. Living in a different world and watching what is going on around you in the real world.

Guilt. Why did you survive and not die with the others? Not worthy of being spared another chance at life.

Shame . More could have been done to help the dying and injured even though all that was possible to have been done was done.

PTSD

Often appear in deep thought. Constantly thinking of those that did not survive or "if only" syndrome.

Introspective (withdrawn). Not wanting to communicate with those around you, just wanting to be left to dwell on past.

Give up activities and past times that used to be enjoyable . Not worthy of being able to enjoy yourself when others have died or been seriously enjoyed.

Depression. A feeling that masks so many other symptoms that makes it difficult for a proper diagnosis to be made, of how you really are. A feeling of wanting to give up, can lead to suicidal thoughts and actions.

Anxiety. Continued state of being fearful of what might happen.

Phobias. Inability to open letters, answer the phone or door, go out on own, visit busy places (supermarkets for example), meet people.

Drug and / or alcohol misuse. Used to escape the world you are caught up in. Use until oblivious. Downside is finding money to supply the addictions, can lead to turning to crime.

Unexplained physical symptoms , sweating, shaking, headaches, dizziness, chest pains Anxiety and worry of how things are going to be in the day, or if experiencing one or more of the phobias.

Anger. Borne out of sheer frustration of how life is and how PTSD is affecting it. The spouse, or close loved ones, is usually the vent of such anger, but can also be "those civilians in authority who do not know what they are doing".

Depression

Depression is a very powerful illness which can mask several other problems such as anxiety as well as taking control as a trigger point.

When feeling depressed there is no future it is just about now. The sufferer is likely to want to self harm. To a great many sufferers they have the power of their own futures, suicidal thoughts can be present. It can be difficult to engage with other people and have any verbal skills. They are marooned on their own island, unable to get back to reality until their pain that caused the depression , can be kept at bay by using medication as well as Therapy. Alcohol or non prescribed drugs can also affect the mood of the sufferer. This is a dangerous and damaging alternative which can lead to all manner of problems.

Depression can last weeks, months and years. The sufferer cannot work properly, and can become a recluse from their friends and family. They stopped enjoying the things they used to and feel worthless, hopeless and constantly tired. Severe depression can lead to suicidal thoughts. One in 10 people suffer with depression at some time in their lives, whilst one in 50 suffer with severe depression.

There is a myriad of tablets available for the symptoms of depression.

Depression can bring about personality changes. These can affect mood swings, anxiety levels, aggression and impulsiveness.

This is not a medical paper if anyone has a mental health problem go to your doctor and seek professional advice.

Numbing and dissociation

Many trauma survivors do all they can to avoid being in triggering situations or relationships in an effort to avoid being hyper aroused.

Instead they numb and shut down, at least partially, or they dissociate. Dissociation is a way to protect yourself from perceived threat and the bad emotions that are associated with what happened to you. Amongst the consequences of numbing are:

Blunted emotional and physical pain, pleasure and responsiveness. Loss of interest in the world and things that previously brought pleasure to you.

Inability to discriminate between pain and pleasure when you do not feel emotions it is easier for you to be re victimized.

Poor memory, clouded thinking.

Lack of emotional responsiveness leading to feelings of shame and the belief that one is shameful.

Increased needs for stimulants and stimulation in order to feel alive; tendency to take risks of all kinds to create excitement and counteract the dead feeling inside you.

Self mutilating as a way to feel alive.

Episodes of panic and rage.

Retreating from life.

Letting your emotional and physical reactions guide you.

Feeling detached from others.

Being unable to experience life, because you feel empty inside.

Having no interest in sex , having sexual dysfunction.

Having no energy, feeling apathetic, and lethargic.

Experiencing mental sluggishness.

PTSD

Gambling and suffering with PTSD

Little is known about post traumatic stress disorder among pathological gamblers even though the two disorders share severe clinical characteristics. The relationship between pathological gambling and post traumatic stress disorder are measures of gambling disorder and severity of experience of specific traumas, psychiatric symptoms, impulsivity and dissociation are both very similar. A total of 149 treatment seeking pathological gamblers were surveyed. Participants were divided into two groups on the basis of their score on the post traumatic stress disorder checklist. Thirty four percent reported a high frequency of post traumatic stress disorder symptoms. Participants who had high scores reported greater lifetime gambling severity, psychiatric symptom, severity impulsivity and dissociation amongst participants who had low post traumatic stress disorder symptom scores. These findings point to a need for more assessment and research about gambling in association with post traumatic stress disorder.

From the emotional tuning .com website the following figures are produced.

PTSD statistics

The following are likely to suffer PTSD to some extent.

30% of armed forces veterans

45% of battered women

50% of sexually abused children

35% of adult rape victims

9.3% service personnel suffered with post traumatic stress disorder before Iraq and it is estimated that 16% will suffer afterwards.

18% of soldiers studied reported they would be too embarrassed to seek mental health services.

24% felt admitting a problem would hurt their careers.

31% felt they would be seen as weak.

38% said they lacked trust in mental health professionals.

In Vietnam for every soldier killed three were injured

In Iraq for every soldier killed seven were injured

In Vietnam roughly 5000 were killed

For every person killed 50 were affected.

PTSD

Children with PTSD

I have deliberately set out some space in this book to deal with the children suffering with PTSD. It is such an unbelievable fact that there are so many children being both physically (sexually) and mentally abused in today's society.

How someone, especially the parents, for example, can do such horrific things to their vulnerable children is beyond belief. It is therefore everyone's responsibility to make sure that when the first signs of abuse become apparent if must be reported to the police or social services to prevent the poor child becoming yet another fatalistic statistic.

If the abuse is detected early enough then hopefully the poor child can go on to live a normal life after a lot of therapy and quite possibly without the parents who may have been the abusers

It's is only by educating those who come into contact with children, will the problems of child abuse be reduced, as well as people taking responsible action and intervention to prevent further hardship to the child.

Children who are abused are far more likely to suffer with PTSD as an adult.

As much as we would like to hope that this was never the case, it is an unfortunate fact of life that there are children today suffering with PTSD. Some of them are in denial which means blocking out the illness for years .Until going through what must be the most terrifying experience imaginable.

Trained soldiers have been known to take their own lives upon returning from battle because of PTS D. So how does a young child have any chance of dealing with it?

Fortunately it is possible to treat a child with PTSD like an adult and enable them to put their lives back together again.

How do you know that a child has PTSD? They might start acting out of character, but when the child is a teenager that could be extremely difficult .If the parents are not the perpetrators, they have a very difficult responsibility in determining what is actually wrong with that child, provided of course that they have heard of and understand PTSD.

The main benchmark is comparing school work or even school itself. There has been a significant and sustained slip in course grades, it could be an indicator something is not right. Similarly if a child consistently plays truant or protests vehemently when taken to school were as previously there was never any problem then something is clearly wrong.

Obviously it might not be PTSD but it could be the precursor to it in later years. Children being sexually abused are more likely to suffer with PTSD as an adult.

In general children display symptoms of depression when suffering with PTSD, but it is not the typical signs that they display.

eating disorders

sleeping patterns, insomnia, oversleeping or nightmares,

constantly tired or overactive

anger

isolation from friends and family,

suicidal thoughts or behaviour. Finding out a child's thoughts can be extremely difficult.

drug or alcohol abuse,

self harming , cutting.

If the child's parents of the perpetrators of the abuse then the responsibility lies with relatives , parents friends, and teachers. It is often the teacher who sees the symptoms and instinctively suspects something unusual is wrong.

The parents or social services should be contacted as the first step towards preventing any abuse continuing, depending on each individual case. Usually the police would be involved if the signs were clearly pointing towards certain adults.

Therapy for a child could be difficult because of the child's limited vocabulary and ability to express themselves. A good therapist will have ways of getting around these problems.

Treatment for PTSD in a child follows the same tools used with an adult, such as C.B.T. and

EMDR as well as medication but depending on the age of the child can include play therapy. The methods of carrying out the therapies in children vary enormously from that of an adult but are just as effective.

Obviously if the parents are the perpetrator then the child will have the extra trauma of not being able to be with them, so ways are found to keep things as calm as possible. A favourite relative could be found or parent of a close friend. In some cases though the child may have to go through the social service system and another home found to live in.

If in any doubt that a child is being abused do not hesitate to act upon that suspicion.

Bereavement

I have included bereavement in order to show that it is not only because of friends and colleagues dying that one mourns, but also the change in circumstance brought about by having PTSD and how it affects the sufferer.

The PTSD sufferer will remember vividly the deaths of those in their Regiment and the anniversary dates. The sufferer will relive those occasions when involved in combat and the level of PTSD will be at its highest. These anniversary dates can often be spread over a year, or more, giving the sufferer little respite from the lead up to one event, thus possibly leaving the sufferer at a continuous state of alertness, on edge and unable to communicate their problems.

If the sufferer is in denial of being in the same battles as their fallen comrades they will try to block out the flashbacks and nightmares by alcohol or drugs which can easily lead to a prison sentence due to aggressive behaviour with alcohol, very common, and dependency on having to fund the addiction to drugs.

With civilians the symptoms present differently. One can be the witness to, or involved in, a car crash, in fact any traumatic event including rape.

It is also possible to be in mourning for the job just lost due to poor timekeeping, attendance, able to do the job when suffering with hangovers. Drugs still present in your system, or redundancy.

This loss of status can be very painful and can remain with the sufferer a long time. Undermining the sufferer's confidence even further still, preventing them from applying for jobs or failing to get a new job because of their lack of confidence, or

PTSD

the glimpse of the chaotic world they transmit over to the interviewer.

For the ex forces personnel who do not want to live off the state, benefits, they face financial ruin if they cannot return to work quickly.

Trigger points that can cause bereavement also include seeing someone dressed as you used to, for example carrying a briefcase, like you used to.

With regard to the ex forces person; not being able to go to his mates for the sheer humiliation felt due to not being able to get a new job.

The bereavement can take the form of crying or the extreme of wanting to self harm.

In my own particular case when I became ill, and had not been diagnosed with PTSD, I found myself crying a great deal whilst thinking of people I knew in the armed forces who have died. I also found myself crying whenever I saw someone in a suit with a briefcase. A few years into my illness my family were invited to a wedding and on the day I was put into a formal suit. By the time I had reached the church I was crying uncontrollably and to my shame in front of my children. I had to be driven back home and missed the entire wedding and reception .It was the thought of wearing a suit and not being able to go back to work, which had been my life.

Anniversaries of battles and close encounters with death are the peak times for breaking down uncontrollably and sobbing endlessly. The nightmares, flashbacks and voices all increase during the anniversary of the event or even the birthday, or wedding date, of those that died.

Fortunately for me I have never suffered with anger so I did not have the problem of containing it. I believe this is due to the violent exposed childhood I had. I realized from a very early age anger is not good and serves no purpose in today's society.

I appreciate that in armed conflict one must have a tremendous, controlled, aggression when dealing with the enemy. Whether this transfers into anger during peacetime is debatable.

I have made a few notes on how to deal with anger and, hopefully, they will help in coming to terms with this dangerous emotion.

PTSD

Anger management

Stop the impulse to act upon an immediate response

Leave the scene

If you think things will get worse walk away

Practice your reactions

Try doing the above when all is well practice helps

Get some exercise

Have a walk or whatever to reduce the adrenaline

Count to three

Do not say the first thing that comes into your mind, delay then think of the consequences of what you want to say.

Admit that there is a problem

Listen to, not hear, what has been said before the eventual reply

Find common ground

No matter how unfair the complaint, or whatever, there is usually some truth in what is being said

Learning how to stop or put the genie back into the bottle

Anyone who has learned how to do things at high-speed hopefully has worked out how to stop in case something went wrong, similarly when dealing with people's problems a good psychiatrist has learned how to safely close a session if it appears too difficult for the patient. I know of someone who suffered because of that inability.

Knowing that this session can be stopped at any time can give the patient a lot more confidence to go further into their memories than they would normally go. If the patient goes into hyper arousal then it is extremely important to be able to deal with this problem.

Hyper arousal can occur when the sympathetic system, responding to situations of danger, threat and stress, go into overdrive exhibiting a pounding heart , dry mouth and the tremors.

Neuroscientists would say that hyper arousal was when there is a flood of adrenaline and other stress related hormones that make a person feel threatened and confused. The brain structures most involved in rational thought and memory, act abnormally.

The two major structures of the limbic system which help the brain deal with danger and emotion are the hippocampus and the amygdala.

The limbic system is central to survival being the area of the mid brain that initiates fight , flight or freeze responses in the face of threat. The hippocampus and the amygdala are deeply involved in responding to traumatic events.

The cortex, the more rational, outermost layer of the brain, is the seat of our thinking capacity and our ability to judge, deliberate, contrast and compare. It is where most memory, traumatic or otherwise is stored. The cortex is in constant communication with the hippocampus and amygdala.

The amygdala is our early warning system. It processes information before the cortex even gets the message something has happened. It could also be the core to post traumatic stress disorder by sending out perpetuating alarms long after the danger has gone.

Along with the amygdala the hippocampus sends messages to the cortex. The hippocampus, however, helps to process information. How well it functions determines the difference between normal and dysfunctional responses to trauma and normal as well as abnormal memory. The hippocampus is highly vulnerable to the stress hormones adrenaline and nor adrenaline, released by the amygdala's alarm. When they reach high levels the hippocampus is unable to function causing a rational evaluation of the situation impossible.

A well functioning hippocampus makes it possible for the cortex to recognize when the trauma is over, perhaps even long gone, and the cortex will then instruct the amygdala to stop sounding the alarm.

The benefits of medication when suffering with PTSD

When a person is really hurting with PTSD taking appropriate tablets can make the world of difference.

Tablets are not for everyone but there are a lot people who benefit from taking them in order to get through the day and, more importantly, through the night.

If you world is spinning out of control and full of suicidal thoughts then tablets can be a rapid solution to the major problem. There will be plenty of time later to come off them.

The problem with PTSD is that it can be so complex that often a cocktail of tablets is required to allow the sufferer some type of normality.

I have realized over the years that PTSD can be a cyclic event, becoming more intense on the anniversary of the tragic events and to this end I reduce my tablets in the relatively easier months and build them back up ready for the not so good months. This is not to say I am cured for six months of the year, just less troubled over a set time. As it happens I have two separate times of PTSD which leave me on a good year one or two months relatively ok, but I never bet on it as there have been any years, this one for example , where my life is just PTSD suffering..

It is generally agreed that tablets cannot cure PTSD but certainly help in relieving the symptoms.

Negative thought patterns

With PTSD it is the negative thought patterns that keep the sufferer trapped with the trauma.

Negative thought patterns have an astonishing power to change lives.

The list of negative thoughts that stem from PTSD is virtually endless, but they can fall into patterns.

Over generalizing

If a person was mugged one may think that all people are cruel yet, if analyzed, it could be shown the person had been walking that way from home the same way and time for over 20 years and this was the only time something had happened.

Always / never

I always fail and never win after an isolated step back, totally surprising to how things usually go.

One-way thinking

Only looking at the negative side of an equation when deciding what to do.

Most of the evidence may show that there is nothing to worry about what you normally decide to do is correct.

CBT can help with thought pattern. (Cognitive Behaviour Therapy)

Analyzing the negative thoughts and putting a realistic approach, and outcome on them. Everyone makes thousands of decisions so there is a chance maybe one decision wasn't the right one. An alternative decision can be made to get around something negative happening.

A simple thought of negativity is thinking that if the telephone rings at three in the morning the first thought could be who has died? It may be that your elderly parent is feeling lonely and just wants to talk. You emigrated abroad years ago and they haven't come to terms with the time difference yet. If the telephone rings next morning at the same time you may think negative thoughts but if it is mum again that may relax you. If the telephone rings the next day at the same time then you could think it is mum again.It would appear there is nothing negative to worry about.

Simple goals to set with CBT

Identify the negative thoughts

Replace them with positive ones

Finding poor behaviour as a result of the negative thoughts and change them.

PTSD

Partners of people with PTSD

When life becomes loveless

You cannot make your partner desire you. Only time and therapy can. This problem needs to be understood to solve it.

To stay or leave

A person with PTSD will often shove their partner away. If you want to spend the rest of your life with them, try to stay connected.

A trial separation rather than a divorce may help.

You are the only one who knows whether a relationship is worth the pain it is putting you through.

No matter how hard you try to overcome the obstacles in trying to keep the marriage going it may prove too much.

Never stay with a partner who is physically or emotionally abusive to yourself or your children.

Children

If at all possible try to talk with your partner when the children are not around as arguments can happen.

Remember children have feelings too and are missing their affected parent.

If there are entrenched family disputes try and discuss them with a family therapist.

The children have suffered enough without them made the bargaining tool when it comes to separation.

The parent returning from combat with PTSD is not the person you married and it is doubtful they will ever be the same again, but bridges can be made and possibilities of the pre combat lifestyle may appear with a lot of patience, hard work and tolerance. The important issue is that you both love each other and must keep talking to each other.

Obsessive Compulsive Disorders in Post Traumatic Stress Disorder

In regard to obsessive compulsive disorder (OCD) specifically, studies have found that anywhere between 4% and 22% of people with PTSD also have a diagnosis of OCD. In addition, people with OCD also show a high likelihood of having experienced traumatic events. For example, one study found that 54% of people with a diagnosis of OCD report having experienced at least one traumatic event in their lifetime. The expedient of traumatic events has also been connected to compulsive behaviours often seen in OCD, such as hoarding, for example, constantly acquiring and not getting rid of a large amount of possessions.

What is OCD? Experience of recurring excessive obsessive activities and mental rituals, as well as repetitive behaviours or thoughts, also called compulsions, such as hand washing, counting, or checking. Obsessions and compulsions commonly defined as:

Obsessions

Obsessions are defined as recurring and persistent thoughts, impulses and or images that are viewed as intrusive and inappropriate. The experience of these thoughts, impulses and/or images, also cause considerable distress and anxiety.

The obsessions in OCD are not just worries about real-life problems and people will try often unsuccessfully to ignore or push away these thoughts, images or impulses. Finally in OCD people recognize that these obsessions are from their own mind and not delusions like that which may be seen in someone with a psychotic disorder.

Compulsions

Compulsions are defined as repetitive behaviours for example excessive hand washing, checking, hoarding, or constantly trying to put things around you in order, or mental rituals for example, frequently praying, counting in your head ,all repeating phrases constantly in your mind. Someone feels like they have to do in response to the experience of obsessive thoughts.

Compulsions are focussed on trying to reduce or eliminate anxiety or prevent the likelihood of some kind of dreaded event or situation.

To have a diagnosis of OCD, a person must experience obsessions and or compulsions, view the obsessions and compulsions as being excessive, unreasonable, and experience considerable distress as a result of having the obsessions and compulsions.

How are PTSD and OCD connected?

In addition to PTSD, people who have experienced a traumatic life event may also be more likely to develop symptoms of OCD. In fact, it has been shown that the severity of the persons OCD symptoms is connected to the number of traumatic events they have experienced in their lifetime.

After experiencing a traumatic event, a person may constantly feel anxious and have concerns about their safety. Compulsive behaviours like checking, ordering or hoarding, may make a person feel in more in control, safe, and reduce anxiety in the short run. However, in the long run, compulsive behaviours do not adequately address the source of the anxiety and can even increase the amount of anxiety someone experiences.

Physical injury

Unlike PTSD this is obvious to everyone the injured person comes into contact with. Because the injuries are usually visible the injured person does not get any respite from well intended people that they come into contact with.

This can bring several problems on a daily, if not hourly, basis as everyone can see the injury for example after stepping on an IED (improvised explosive device).

The injured person can have no respite from the injury it is always there for them and all to see.

It would not be unknown for the injured person to have PTSD, reliving the time the explosion happened. Why me? There are times when sleep will not come to the injured because of their mental condition. It is extremely likely that the injured person would take some of the boxes that go to make up PTSD.

PTSD in people with learning difficulties

People with learning disabilities are at greater risk for psychiatric disorder than the general population (1970). Individuals with mild to profound learning disability as a sufferer, presents disorders similar to those affecting the more able population. The main difficulty is diagnosis, as the presentations of disorder may be different than those with severe developmental delay. Therefore, the diagnosis of PTSD than those who do not have the communication skills to describe the thoughts, feelings and mood may be hindered. At times we are reliant on observing changes in behaviour and function, for example, aggression, regressive behaviours and changes in sleep patterns. Owing to the limited recognition of PTSD in people with learning disability the symptoms may be attributed to other psychiatric diagnoses.

In considering the nature of the psycho pathology following that which caused the traumatic stress in those with learning disability, it needs to be recognized that neurotic / anxiety disorders and adjustment disorders are still unknown quantities. One study of anxiety disorders (1997) shows the prevailing symptoms to be aggression, agitation, self injurious behaviour, obsessive fears and insomnia with specific symptoms of panic attacks, agoraphobia, sexual dysfunction, made changes, depersonalization, and derealisation. Of 70 patients presenting with the symptoms 63 had experienced one or more of the following events in the past 3 to 6 months: rape/ sexual assault, physical assault, accident, illness , a move, bereavement or change in care. Therefore, it is not unusual for anxiety disorders to be preceded by a traumatic event in those with learning disability.

Grief in adults with learning disability is often accompanied by an increase in anxiety symptoms and abhorrent behaviours, without improvements over time, particularly in the anxiety symptoms (1999).

There has been only one reported major study of adults with learning disability diagnosed to have PTSD (1994). This was a clinical population of 51 adults and showed that people with learning disability develop PTSD at a rate comparable to the population when exposed to trauma. Each person had suffered at least two types of trauma. That most frequently experienced was sexual abuse by multiple perpetrators which was commonly started in childhood, physical abuse or life threatening neglect committed some other active abuse of trauma. A few cases did not include abuse: for example, a sibling dying in a fire, seeing a close friend die during a seizure, or witnessing a parent commit suicide by gunshot wounds to the head. All those cases of trauma involved seeing a carer, friend or close relative die in traumatic circumstances.

Almost all people with learning disabilities are at greater risk for psychiatric disorder than the general population (1970). Individuals with mild to profound learning disability suffer disorders similar to those affecting the more able population.

Recovery

Recovery can mean lots of different levels to lots of different people pages

It does not have to mean being able to go back to work and push the managing director out of his chair as you think you can do it now.

To some people recovery could mean being able to go outside the house and walk around the supermarket buy the shopping and return home without any problems.

There are people who suffer with PTSD who may never be able to achieve that, but feel as though they have recovered because they can take the dog for a walk around the local park.

Depending on what initiated the trauma, which can take a very long time in counselling to get to, it can ultimately depend on what type of recovery is managed and maintained.

A great part of counselling is the counsellor understanding the realistic goals and working together on the agreed goals. There is no point going down the London underground if you have a terror of enclosed spaces and a fear of people. It may be more beneficial that you go out on your own travel on the bus on an off peak quiet time. This would be a huge achievement and something that could be repeated without causing a relapse in your state of health.

It is extremely important to remember that when ill one normally compares how they are then with how well one was in one's prime. For example someone who has developed a knee injury and can barely walk 100 yards without crutches thinks back to when they ran 5 miles before breakfast.

PTSD

There are three main stages of Recovery:

The victim: the trauma takes over your life and takes everything away from you. It is impossible to be rational about things and only the pain and bad exist.

The survivor: the stage when the trauma is still recalled , yet there is a structure to the day and decisions can be made without fear of the bad days returning. Providing everything is done in moderation and avoiding trigger points are in place for improving your quality of life and not bringing back the horror that made-up PTSD.

Just because you now only need five tablets to get you through the day when you used to need 10 does not mean you're better. You are taking tablets because you are still not well. Do not forget the tablets alone are not a cure for PTSD.

The Thriver: things have become more or less normal again and you have returned to the way of doing things you did, in moderation, before PTSD.

There is a stage during the Recovery process that being told that " you look better today", doesn't mean that you have fully recovered but that you seem to be coping better than a while ago. Many sufferers of PTSD are fearful of such a statement because they know how they are, and what is happening to them on the inside. To be told they are better, which although not said but that is how the sufferers interpret the observation, the fear is so intense that it can make the sufferer worse than they have been for a while and knock them a few steps back on their road to recovery.

Being thought of as better...........able to return to work? Certainly not how the sufferer feels and is so afraid that they are thought of as better and they can return to work, has the sufferers brain racing so fast they can see all different types of outcome by "being signed off the sick".

It is extremely important that those who come into contact with PTSD sufferers be very careful in choosing their words when talking to them, or let the sufferer lead the way and follow how the conversation goes.

There are times though, contrary to the above, that the PTSD sufferer is in mourning for their previous job, either in the forces or in civvy street, that they fool themselves out of sheer desperation "to be normal "again and will say anything to try and return to how they were before their trauma, and it is at this stage that the trained psychiatric professionals must understand what is actually going on and prevent the sufferer from attempting to return in order to have a far greater relapse and feel a lot worse than they really were.

PTSD

Sleep with PTSD

It's is common for sufferers of PTSD to experience sleep problems. Difficulty with getting off to sleep and or staying asleep is considered one of the hyper arousal symptoms of PTSD and it is most commonly reported by PTSD sufferers.

If the sufferer managed to get to sleep the vast majority experience nightmares. These nightmares are like daytime flashbacks with them being so vivid and the sense of being there so real it's is quite common to smell the scene and feel the intense heat.

Poor sleep can lead to contributing to stress and mood swings. It can also have a negative effect on physical health. It is usual for there to be an overlap between sleep and awake, resulting in hallucinations and confusion of what is actually happening.

Aids to help sleep

Exercise

Regular sleep patterns

Avoid eating heavy meals before going to bed

Reduce caffeine and nicotine

Avoid naps throughout the day

Avoid alcohol six hours before sleep

Do not try to force yourself to sleep

Practice relaxation exercises

Trying to separate worries from sleep

Use prescribed medication

As can be clearly seen from the above list it would be in an ideal world where one would be able to do what has been suggested, when dealing with a person who has PTSD and probably alcohol or drug addiction as well, their life already in ruin, they are all alone and have no structure or motivation to do anything except look for the means of funding their next fix, and their lives just simply does not exist beyond that. It can be clearly seen that it is practically impossible to carry out a formal and sustained approach to dealing with sleep. The closest the sufferer gets to sleep is probably unconsciousness through taking drugs.

It is quite common for a PTSD sufferer to become paranoid whilst in a state of alcohol or drugs abuse. They believe they are being followed by someone or something that lies in the shadows and is ready to attack him when their defences are down. It can be for this reason that a variety of street drugs may be used, to heighten arousal and keep the sufferer awake despite their body's need for sleep. It's obvious that this cannot go on indefinitely and sooner or later they crash out and suffer with the nightmares that their PTSD will bring them.

Sleep apnea

A study was done in the USA with people having breathing disorders during the night and suffering nightmares from PTSD. When the disorder was treated to a manageable level, it was found that there was a 75% improvement in Apnea .Sleep disorders included loud and prolonged snoring, thrashing around during sleep, nightmares and fatigue joining the day. Sleep apnea is very treatable by a GP and once treated reduce high blood pressure as well as reduce the risk of a heart attack and stroke.

What do I say to the person who says they have PTSD?

It would be highly unusual for someone to say they have post traumatic stress disorder unless there was cause to do so. Generally sufferers want to fit in with the crowd and be anonymous. However there might be reason for them to do so.

If the person was having an episode that appeared unusual and was coming out of that episode they realized you looked shocked or quizzical.

It's is quite common for sufferers to have flashbacks of the events which may make them appear distant. Depending on the confidence and the point on the road to recovery the sufferer is at, they may say what has happened.

Do not treat them as infirm or reassure them all will be okay.

They are not and it will not be. Things may improve at best.

Do not tell them that they are strange, they are not. They are perfectly normal but have an illness that is difficult to deal with and treat.

A more positive approach would be to say" sorry but I noticed what you were like just then is there anything I can do to help?"

Sometimes a glass of water is helpful as the body and mind are badly affected by flashbacks.

If a person starts talking incoherently then do not be alarmed they are probably talking to the people who make up that PTSD and have visited them.

Overall the plan is to act as normal as possible and try not to embarrass the sufferer anymore than they feel already.

PTSD

Ten myths about PTSD

Only armed forces personnel suffer with PTSD

Having PTSD is a sign of weakness

Time alone will heal it.

Therapy will heal all your problems

Blocking out the trauma is easier than facing them

It's gone on too long to be PTSD

PTSD causes violence

You deserve PTSD

You cannot afford time for therapy

PTSD isn't real

"I pray you to believe what I have said. I reported what I saw and heard, but only part of it. For most of it I have no words."

Ed Munrow Buchanswald 1945

Epilogue

I hope that by reading this book many PTSD sufferers will be able to relate to what I have written, as well as the never to be forgotten Carers, who do a magnificent job through the good and terrible times.

I have stated earlier that professionals, working in the mental health system, who come across a PTSD sufferer for the first time, may gain an insight into the tortuous world of PTSD and help them understand what the sufferer is probably going through.

The book is not meant to be a definitive article but just a glimpse at PTSD, which may lead the reader to go on to read more definitive books, if this happens then the writing of this has been worthwhile.

It is my intention that the book be a brief and easy to refer to introduction to the world of PTSD and stimulate readers into wanting to find out more. There is so much more that I could have written about the subject, and maybe in the fullness of time that will come to pass.

It has been a very difficult book to write with many memories flooding back of my own PTSD problems, some I had completely forgotten about, but I thought that by writing them down it would minimise their effect on me. Unfortunately this did not always prove to be the case.

There were some subjects new to me, such as dealing with young children and those with learning difficulties that were particularly difficult to come to terms with.

The most shocking part of the book, for myself, were the statistics and the sheer number of sufferers who really need more help and guidance, as well as their Carers who often carry out their role unpaid and having had to make great sacrifices, in order to do their part in looking after the sufferer to the best of their ability.

Glossary of terms

Acceptance and Commitment Therapy

Suffering that comes from attempted avoidance of that pain which is only effective in the short term may cause greater problems in the long term. Helps to enable people have their experiences told as they are more open about their experiences.

Acute Stress Disorder

an anxiety disorder that can develop immediately following a traumatic incident. To qualify the person must have had a traumatic event where there was a threat of death or serious injury and the strong feeling of fear.

Anxiety Disorder

a large class of mental disorders that includes several disorders involving various problems associated with the experience of fear and anxiety .Post Traumatic Stress Disorder being one.

Anxiety Sensitivity

a person's tendency to fear anxiety related symptoms e.g. increasing heart rate being one

Avoidance Symptoms

Avoidance symptoms of PTSD e.g. thoughts places feelings. Distance from others.

Complex PTSD

Exposure to chronic longer-lasting traumatic events May suffer from more than one traumatic event. Sexual abuse as a child and witness to a traumatic event as an adult , for example.

Defence Mechanisms

Avoiding painful feelings in the conscious mind, stemming from a traumatic experience.

EMDR

Eye movement desensitization and reprocessing therapy

Where a sufferer confronts and works through their original trauma, it helps the sufferer replace self destructive ideas with beneficial ones using eye movement, following the examiner's finger movement at the same time as recalling the traumatic event.

Flashback

A re- experiencing of symptoms of PTSD.

A person feels or acts as though a traumatic event is happening again. The smell and sound are prevalent.

Grounding

A variant of mindfulness using the five senses to ground to the present moment.

Hippocampus

Part of the limbic system in the brain is able to store and retrieve memory. Can shrink by up to 20% of normal size in a PTSD sufferer.

Hyper arousal

A specific cluster of symptoms that stem from high levels of anxiety.

Hyper vigilance

One of the hyper arousal symptoms being constantly tense and on guard.

Panic attack

The experience of intense fear with four or five of symptoms being present, palpitations, sweat, trembling, being smothered, choking etc.

Post Traumatic Stress Disorder

A witness to, or participant in, a traumatic event which has left a sense of trauma. Not usually evident until weeks, months or years later. It can last from weeks to lifetime.

Relapse

The worsening of the condition, or the reoccurrence of unhealthy behaviour by avoidance and substance abuse.

Survivor guilt

A strong feeling of guilt of having survived a trauma that had fatalities.

Trigger

Anything that brings about the symptoms of Post Traumatic Stress Disorder.

www.ingramcontent.com/pod-product-compliance
Ingram Content Group UK Ltd.
Pitfield, Milton Keynes, MK11 3LW, UK
UKHW041412180426
11947UKWH00007B/94